SUPERMAN

and the
Mischief
on Mars

A SOLAR SYSTEM ADVENTURE

by Steve Korté
illustrated by Gregg Schigiel

Superman created by Jerry Siegel and Joe Shuster
by special arrangement with the Jerry Siegel family

Consultant:
Steve Kortenkamp, PhD
Associate Professor of Practice
Lunar and Planetary Lab
University of Arizona
Tucson, Arizona

CAPSTONE PRESS
a capstone imprint

Professor Emil Hamilton watches a large screen at the famous scientific laboratory S.T.A.R. Labs. The screen shows videos taken by an unmanned spacecraft on Mars. The fourth planet from the Sun is a dead desert world, so the professor is a little bored. Suddenly, his mouth falls open in surprise.

"Something is moving on the planet's surface!" he says, pointing to the screen. "Are those tiny red people? Impossible!"

Hamilton jumps to his feet and reaches for a phone.

"I need to ask Superman to come to the lab immediately," he says. "Maybe he can get to the bottom of this mystery."

Superman quickly flies to S.T.A.R. Labs. The hero studies the image on the video screen.

"Incredible," he says. "I thought life couldn't exist on Mars."

"That's right," says Hamilton. "Liquid water is essential for life. But water on Mars is mostly in the form of ice or vapor."

"Was there ever life on Mars, Professor?" asks Superman.

"Perhaps," says Hamilton. "Mars is covered in dry riverbeds. That suggests water once flowed on the planet billions of years ago. And if there was liquid water, there may have been life. But there isn't any evidence of life that is widely accepted by scientists."

FACT
In 2020 NASA plans to launch a rover called *Mars 2020*. It will search for chemical evidence of past life within the Martian soil.

Hamilton switches the image. The Red Planet fills the screen.

"Mars is generally very cold, but the surface temperature can vary," he says. "It can be as cold as minus 225 degrees Fahrenheit, or minus 143 degrees Celsius. But at the equator, the temperature can reach 70 degrees Fahrenheit, or 20 degrees Celsius. The planet's atmosphere is mostly made of carbon dioxide. There isn't enough oxygen for humans to breathe."

"So the figures we saw in that video are *not* from Earth," Superman says. "I think I need to take a trip to Mars, Professor. Do you have a map of the planet I can borrow?"

Superman steps outside S.T.A.R. Labs and launches himself into the air.

ZOOOOM!

He travels through Earth's atmosphere and past the Moon. Mars is the next planet out from Earth, but the Man of Steel still has a long journey. On average, a distance of about 140 million miles (225 million kilometers) separates the two planets.

Eventually, he sees Deimos and Phobos, the two small moons that orbit Mars.

Superman flies past Deimos. The moon has a lumpy shape and is less than 8 miles (13 km) wide. Its rocky surface is dotted with craters.

FACT

Long ago, Phobos and Deimos may have been asteroids. They may have been pulled closer to Mars by the planet's gravity and then captured as moons.

Superman flies away from Deimos and heads closer toward Mars. Soon he is soaring over the planet's frozen north pole. Giant, swirling dunes cover the area. Each dune is sculpted out of wind-blown sand that lies on top of bright white ice.

Superman zooms over the planet's many canyons and mountains. He sees long, winding holes in the ground that look like dry riverbeds. Huge boulders are scattered across the surface.

Soon the Man of Steel arrives at the giant canyon known as Valles Marineris. He soars high over its cliffs and then dives toward its dusty red floor.

This was where the mysterious tiny red Martians had last been spotted.

FACT
Valles Marineris is 2,500 miles (4,000 km) long and stretches about a quarter of the way around Mars. It's ten times longer and five times deeper than the Grand Canyon in Arizona.

Superman lands on the red, rocky surface of Mars.

"*Chaaaaaaarge!*" a voice says.

Seven tiny figures suddenly run out from behind a boulder and head straight toward Superman. But the little beings aren't human. Each one is made of Martian rocks. They're completely red from head to toe.

Before Superman can react, all seven crash into him.

BLAM!

The rock people crumble into tiny piles of red dust.

FACT
The red dust covering Mars' surface is made up of iron oxide, which is basically rust.

"What in the world . . . ," says Superman, but then he hears another noise.

A loud voice cackles with high-pitched laughter.

Superman follows the sound behind a large red rock. He discovers the voice belongs to Mr. Mxyzptlk, the magical imp from the Fifth Dimension who loves to cause trouble.

"Mxy! I might have known," says Superman with a frown.

The super hero knows there's only one way to send the imp back to the Fifth Dimension. Mr. Mxyzptlk has to be tricked into saying his own name backward.

"What are you doing here?" Superman asks sternly.

"I decided to create my own Martians so I could have a little company here," replies Mr. Mxyzptlk. "But I guess my rocky friends weren't very sturdy."

"Enough tricks," says Superman. "It's time for you to—"

"This planet is pretty dull and dusty, don't you think?" interrupts Mxy. He yawns and looks around. "I bet I can make it more interesting. I think I'll start with the Asteroid Belt."

POOF!

The imp disappears in a cloud of white smoke.

Superman groans and flies away from the Red Planet.

He knows millions of small rocky objects called asteroids orbit the Sun. Most of them are located in the Asteroid Belt between Mars and Jupiter.

Superman arrives in the Asteroid Belt and looks around. Thousands of rocks zoom past him. Some are smaller than an inch. Others are hundreds of miles wide.

What is Mxy up to? wonders Superman.

Superman finally spots Mr. Mxyzptlk hard at work in the middle of the Asteroid Belt. The imp uses his magic to move a huge asteroid out of its regular orbit. He brings it over to the Red Planet.

"Let's see if I can crash this big rock into Mars," says Mxy. "I think it would be fun to make a new crater!"

The prankster laughs as he sends the asteroid spinning toward Mars.

ZAAAAAAP!

Red-hot lasers shoot out of
Superman's eyes. The Man of Steel
uses his heat-vision to smash the
giant asteroid into tiny bits.

15

"You're ruining all my fun, you big Super-Spoiler!" shouts Mr. Mxyzptlk. He zooms to the Asteroid Belt again. "I'm going to cast a spell to—"

Before the imp can finish his sentence, Superman uses his super-breath. He blows a big asteroid straight toward the villain.

"Uh-oh!" cries Mxy.

Seconds before the asteroid crashes into him, Mxy makes a quick decision.

"No fair!" he declares. "I'm going back to Mars!"

POOF!

The outraged imp disappears again.

Superman quickly zaps the asteroid with his heat-vision so it won't cause any future problems. With a sigh, the Man of Steel heads back toward Mars.

Superman finds Mr. Mxyzptlk on the planet's northern polar cap. The huge white area is made up of ice, sand, and dust.

"I know what's wrong with Mars," says the imp. "It's too dry! How about if I melt some of this ice and make a water park? Doesn't that sound like fun?"

Superman flies closer to Mxy. He wants to grab the trickster before he can cast a spell.

"Not so fast," says the imp. "You need to chill out!"

WHOOOOSH!

Mr. Mxyzptlk magically creates a blizzard that sends Superman flying backward.

With Superman out of the way, Mr. Mxyzptlk waves his arms. Magical red and yellow flames slice through the polar cap. A huge chunk of ice melts into a raging river of water.

It's the first time in billions of years that water has flowed on this part of Mars. Mxy laughs in delight.

But then Mr. Mxyzptlk frowns.

Despite the imp's magic, liquid water can't remain for long on the dry world of Mars. Every drop of water quickly evaporates.

With a sigh of frustration, Mxy turns back to the polar ice cap. He gets ready to melt more ice.

FACT

Frozen water exists on Mars, but liquid water cannot last on the planet's surface. The planet's thin atmosphere of carbon dioxide keeps water from forming.

VROOOOOM!

Superman swoops in and sends a gust of his freeze-breath straight toward Mr. Mxyzptlk.

"Hey, what's the big idea—" begins Mxy.

But Mxy is now completely trapped inside a thick ice cube. His mouth is still wide open in the middle of his question.

"Stay cool, Mxy," says Superman with a smile.

The Man of Steel picks up the ice cube.

"I know how you love to travel, Mxy," says Superman. He pulls back his arm and throws the ice cube into space with all his strength.

The frozen imp sails far, far away.

The Man of Steel knows that the ice won't hold Mxy for long. He needs a plan to get rid of the troublesome trickster. He reaches into a pouch within his cape and takes out Professor Hamilton's map. He has an idea.

Minutes later, Mr. Mxyzptlk returns to Mars. He flies past the Man of Steel.

"I've got a new idea," he calls out to Superman. "In fact, this one is going to be a blast. You're just going to lava it!"

"*Blast? Lava?*" Superman says to himself. Then he realizes what the imp is planning.

Mxy is going to make a Martian volcano erupt!

Superman finds Mr. Mxyzptlk floating above the volcano Olympus Mons, which stands 16 miles (26 km) high.

"I hear this is the tallest volcano on any of the planets in your solar system," says Mxy. "Let's see if a little lava—maybe a billion tons or so—will spice up Mars."

Superman takes out Hamilton's map again. He studies it carefully.

"Your information is out of date, Mxy," says the Man of Steel. "According to this map, there's another volcano on Mars that's even taller."

The outraged imp flies over to Superman. "A taller volcano? Show me!" he demands.

The instant Mr. Mxyzptlk says his name backward, he disappears. The imp has returned to the Fifth Dimension.

Superman sighs with relief as he soars toward Earth. He uses a small radio inside his cape to report back to Professor Hamilton.

"Did you solve the Martian mystery?" asks Hamilton.

"As I suspected, Mr. Mxyzptlk was behind it," says Superman. "But your map proved handy."

"How so?" asks Hamilton.

"While Mxy was on ice, I used my heat-vision to burn his name backward onto the Mars map," the hero replies. "I'm afraid I ruined your map, though."

"No worries, Superman," says Hamilton with a laugh. "It was for a good cause!"

MORE ABOUT MARS

- We don't know who first recognized Mars was a planet. Astronomers in ancient Egypt were writing about the planet as early as 1500 BC.

- The planet's red color visible in Earth's nighttime sky reminded ancient people of blood and violence. So it was named Mars after the Roman god of war.

- Winds on the surface of Mars can reach 185 miles (298 km) per hour. The strong winds pick up the red dust on the ground and blow it into the atmosphere. These dust storms can cover the entire planet and last for months at a time.

- Mars is the second smallest planet in the solar system. It's roughly half the size of Earth.

- A Martian day lasts 24 hours, 39 minutes, and 23 seconds. It takes Mars almost 669 Martian days (or about 687 Earth days) to orbit the Sun.

- The moon Phobos is moving closer to Mars at a rate of about 6 feet (1.8 m) every century. In about 50 million years Phobos could crash into the planet or break into pieces.

- The moon Deimos is moving slowly away from Mars. In millions of years it may escape Mars' gravity and float away into space.

- Seven unmanned spacecraft have landed successfully on Mars. The *Sojourner* spacecraft was the first roving vehicle, touching down in 1997. It's still on the planet but no longer active.

- The most recent rover to land on Mars was *Curiosity* in 2012. Its mission is to collect rock and soil samples to see if Mars was ever able to support life. One sample showed Mars had liquid water long ago.

- Several nations, including China, Russia, and the United States, are working to send the first humans to Mars by the 2030s or 2040s. Some private companies are also working toward this goal. Most programs are still in the planning stages.

GLOSSARY

asteroid (AS-tuh-royd)—a large chunk of space rock that moves around the Sun

atmosphere (AT-muhss-fihr)—the layer of gases that surrounds some planets, dwarf planets, and moons

crater (KRAY-tuhr)—a hole made when asteroids and comets crash into a planet's or moon's surface

dimension (duh-MEN-shuhn)—a different place in space and time

dune (DOON)—a hill or ridge of sand piled up by the wind

evaporate (ih-VA-puh-rayt)—to change from a liquid to a gas

gravity (GRAV-uh-tee)—a force that pulls objects together

Mxyzptlk (mix-ee-YEZ-pit-uhl-ick)—an imp from the Fifth Dimension who likes to play tricks on others

orbit (OR-bit)—to travel around an object in space; also the path an object follows while circling another object in space

rover (ROH-vur)—a small vehicle that people can move by using remote control; rovers are used to explore objects in space

solar system (SOH-lur SISS-tuhm)—the Sun and the objects that move around it

READ MORE

Aguilar, David A. *Seven Wonders of the Solar System*. New York: Viking, 2017.

Radomski, Kassandra. *The Secrets of Mars*. Planets. North Mankato, Minn.: Capstone Press, 2016.

Silverman, Buffy. *Mars Missions*. Space Discovery Guides. Minneapolis, Minn.: Lerner Publications, 2017.

TITLES IN THIS SET

INDEX

INTERNET SITES

Use FactHound to find Internet sites related to this book.
Visit *www.facthound.com*
Just type in 9781543515633 and go.

Published by Capstone Press in 2018
1710 Roe Crest Drive
North Mankato, Minnesota 56003
www.mycapstone.com

Cataloging-in-publication information is on file with the Library of Congress.
ISBN 978-1-5435-1563-3 (library binding)
ISBN 978-1-5435-1575-6 (paperback)
ISBN 978-1-5435-1583-1 (eBook PDF)

Editorial Credits
Abby Huff, editor; Kyle Grenz, designer; Laura Manthe, production specialist

Summary: Superman chases after the troublesome imp Mr. Mxyzptlk and along the way discovers
remarkable features and characteristics of Mars and the Asteroid Belt.

Illustration Credits
Dario Brizuela: front cover, back cover (space), 1 (space), 28–29, 30–31, 32 (space)

Printed in the United States of America.
PA017